CELEBRATE CHRISTMAS WITH PAPER CRAFTS

Randel
McGee

Enslow Elementary

an imprint of

Enslow Publishers, Inc.

40 Industrial Road
Box 398
Berkeley Heights, NJ 07922
USA

http://www.enslow.com

Dedicated to Marsha the Supreme Santa Supporter and Nathan, Melanie, Adam, Matthew, and Aaron, Elves Extraordinaire and Keepers of the Santa Secrets, AND to my newest grandchild, Mable Rose Evans.

This book meets the National Standards for Arts Education.

Enslow Elementary, an imprint of Enslow Publishers, Inc.
Enslow Elementary® is a registered trademark of Enslow Publishers, Inc.

Library of Congress Cataloging-in-Publication Data

McGee, Randel.
 [Paper crafts for Christmas]
 Celebrate Christmas with paper crafts / Randel McGee.
   pages cm — (Celebrate holidays with paper crafts)
 Audience: Grades K to grade 3.
 Revised edition of: Paper crafts for Christmas.
 Includes bibliographical references and index.
 ISBN 978-0-7660-6355-6 (hardback) — ISBN 978-0-7660-6356-3 (paperback) — ISBN 978-0-7660-6357-0 (EPUB) — ISBN 978-0-7660-6358-7 (Single-user PDF) — ISBN 978-0-7660-6359-4 (multi-user PDF) 1. Christmas decorations—Juvenile literature. 2. Paper work—Juvenile literature. I. Title.
 TT900.C4M38 2015
 745.594'12—dc23
                          2014025027

Summary: "Discusses the history of Christmas and how to make eight holiday-themed paper crafts"—Provided by publisher.

Future editions:
Paperback ISBN: 978-0-7660-6356-3
Single-User PDF ISBN: 978-0-7660-6358-7

EPUB ISBN: 978-0-7660-6357-0
Multi-User PDF ISBN: 978-0-7660-6359-4

Printed in the United States of America

102014 Bang Printing, Brainerd, Minn.

10 9 8 7 6 5 4 3 2 1

To Our Readers: We have done our best to make sure all Internet addresses in this book were active and appropriate when we went to press. However, the author and the publisher have no control over and assume no liability for the material available on those Internet sites or on other Web sites they may link to. Any comments or suggestions can be sent by e-mail to comments@enslow.com or to the address on the back cover.

♻ Enslow Publishers, Inc., is committed to printing our books on recycled paper. The paper in every book contains 10% to 30% post-consumer waste (PCW). The cover board on the outside of each book contains 100% PCW. Our goal is to do our part to help young people and the environment, too!

Illustration Credits: Crafts prepared by Randel McGee and photos on pp. 27, 28, 47; craft photography by Nicole diMella/Enslow Publishers, Inc.; Shutterstock.com: Atelier Sommerland, p. 4; Victorian Traditions, p. 5.

Cover Illustration: Crafts prepared by Randel McGee; craft photography by Nicole diMella/Enslow Publishers, Inc.

Contents

AUTHOR'S NOTE: Many of the materials used in making these crafts may be found by using recycled paper products. The author uses such recycled items as cereal boxes and similar packaging for light cardboard, manila folders for card stock paper, leftover pieces of wrapping paper, and so forth. This not only reduces the cost of the projects but is also a great way to reuse and recycle paper. Be sure to ask an adult for permission before using any recycled paper products.

The projects in this book were created for this particular holiday. However, I invite readers to be imaginative and find new ways to use the ideas in this book to create different projects of their own. Please feel free to share pictures of your work with me through www.mcgeeproductions.com. Happy crafting!

CHRISTMAS!

Christmas is a Christian holiday that celebrates the birth of Jesus Christ about two thousand years ago. It is a day that honors one very special event, and yet wherever it is celebrated, there are special customs for celebrating this holiday.

More than three hundred years after the birth of Jesus Christ, the Roman Catholic Church set December 25 as the date to celebrate this event. They called it "Christ's Mass," which was later shortened to Christmas. December 25 was a special date in many European cultures, as they celebrated the return of the sun after the long dark days of winter. Each culture added their own mid-winter customs to their celebration of Christmas. Some of the old customs that were brought to the Christmas celebration were decorating homes with branches from holly and fir trees and mistletoe.

The Germans had a tradition of celebrating Christmas by setting up a small fir tree in their homes and decorating it with small candles. The tree and candles were reminders of everlasting life and light. Small gifts and sweets were also hung on the tree as decorations for the children to enjoy. The German immigrants who came to America brought with them the tradition of the decorated Christmas tree.

The Dutch people who came to America brought with them a tradition of a special gift giver, named Sint Niklaas, or Saint Nicholas in English, who would deliver gifts to good children. Saint Nicholas was a bishop in Turkey. He was known for his good deeds and generosity. There is a legend that Saint Nicholas placed some coins in the stockings of poor children who had hung them by the fire to dry. The custom of putting presents in stockings as a gift from St. Nicholas became a part of the American Christmas tradition. Dutch children called him Sinterklaas. American children called him Santa Claus.

The American tradition of Santa Claus as the Christmas gift giver started in the early 1800s. In 1809, the well-known author Washington

Irving wrote about Santa Claus as a fat little man who rode through the air in a sleigh pulled by reindeer. Then in 1822, Clement Clarke Moore, a minister and teacher, wrote a poem for his children that he called "A Visit From Saint Nicholas," more commonly known as "The Night Before Christmas." He used Irving's description of Santa Claus and his sleigh pulled by reindeer. He created Santa's ability to go up and down a chimney as if by magic. The poem was published the next year and became very popular. In the late 1800s, a famous illustrator named Thomas Nast made hundreds of cartoons of Santa Claus based on the poem by Clement Clarke Moore. Nast's pictures became the images of Santa that most Americans recognize today.

A British author had a great effect on the way people celebrate Christmas. In 1843, Charles Dickens wrote *A Christmas Carol*. This story about mean, old Ebenezer Scrooge, who was visited by three spirits on Christmas Eve, inspired people around the world to look at Christmas as a special time of friendship and caring. *A Christmas Carol* is still one of the most popular Christmas stories.

So on your walls hang wreaths of holly!
Make a little Santa Claus that's jolly!
Give a little Christmas cheer when you craft a small reindeer!
Send your friends a Christmas greeting or invite them to a festive meeting.
Place ornaments for all to see, add an angel atop your Christmas tree.
'Tis the season for paper and scissors! Don't wait!
Christmas is coming! So let's decorate!

O CHRISTMAS TREE

There is a legend that Martin Luther, a famous German church leader and writer of the 1500s, was walking home one winter night and was impressed with the beauty of a fir tree with stars sparkling through its branches. He cut a small fir tree and brought it into his home. He placed little candles on its branches to represent the stars. He showed it to his friends and family as a symbol of life and light. Christmas trees became an important part of the German holiday celebration that was brought to America with the German immigrants. "O Christmas Tree" ("O Tannenbaum" in German) is a well-known Christmas carol. Here is a little Christmas tree for you to decorate.

WHAT YOU WILL NEED

- tracing paper
- pencil
- green construction paper
- scissors
- markers or crayons
- glitter (optional)
- glitter glue (optional)
- construction paper scraps
- white glue
- stapler
- clear tape
- card stock (optional)

WHAT TO DO

1. Use the tracing paper to transfer the pattern from page 37 to the green construction paper (See A). Make four trees. Cut them out.

A)

2. Decorate the four tree shapes as you wish with markers, crayons, glitter, or little ornaments made from scraps of construction paper (See B). Let dry.

B)

3. Put the four tree shapes together on top of each other (See C). Staple all four trees together down the middle from top to bottom.

C)

4. Fold each side of the pattern a little along the stapled line so that the sides open out to form a tree.

5. Tape the bottom edges of the finished tree to a sheet of construction paper or card stock to make it stand.

HOLLY WREATH

The holly is an evergreen plant, meaning that it still has leaves on it in the winter. People in ancient times thought that holly had the power to chase away evil spirits. The spiky leaves and bright red berries of the holly remind Christians of the crown of thorns placed on Jesus's head. Both evergreen branches and the circle shape of the wreath are symbols of everlasting life.

WHAT YOU WILL NEED

- tracing paper
- pencil
- green and red construction paper
- scissors
- ruler
- one 9-inch paper plate
- white glue
- ribbon
- clear tape

WHAT TO DO

1. Use tracing paper to transfer the holly leaf pattern to the green construction paper and the berry pattern to the red construction paper. (See page 35 for the patterns.) Make twenty leaves and twenty berries. Cut out all the pieces (See A).

2. Carefully cut a circle, about 6 inches across, out of the center of the paper plate and throw it away, leaving a ring to serve as a base for your wreath (See B).

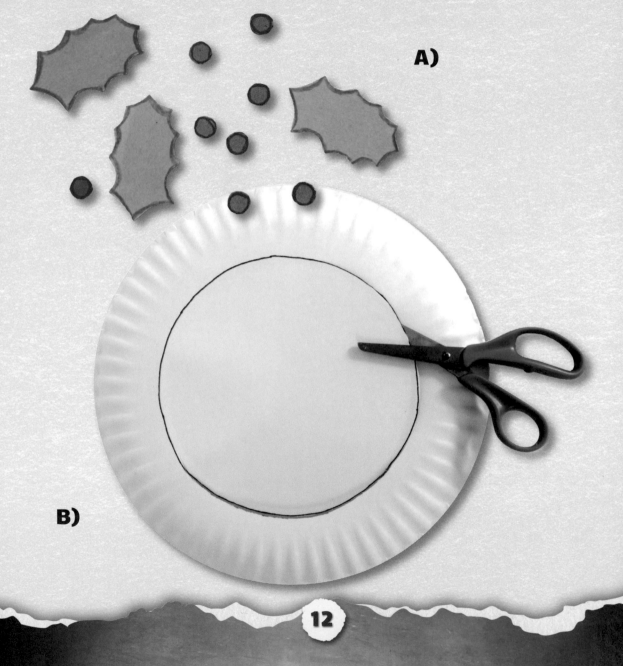

A)

B)

3. Glue the holly leaves to the paper plate ring. Start at the bottom of one side of the plate and overlap the leaves a little bit until you reach the top (See C). Do the same on the other side of the circle. Let dry.

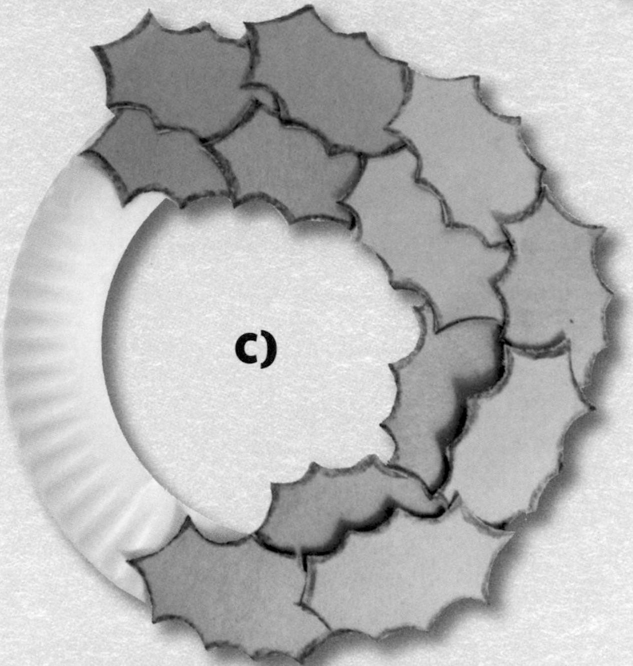

C)

4. Glue the red berries in little groups of two or three around the wreath on top of the leaves (See D). Let dry.

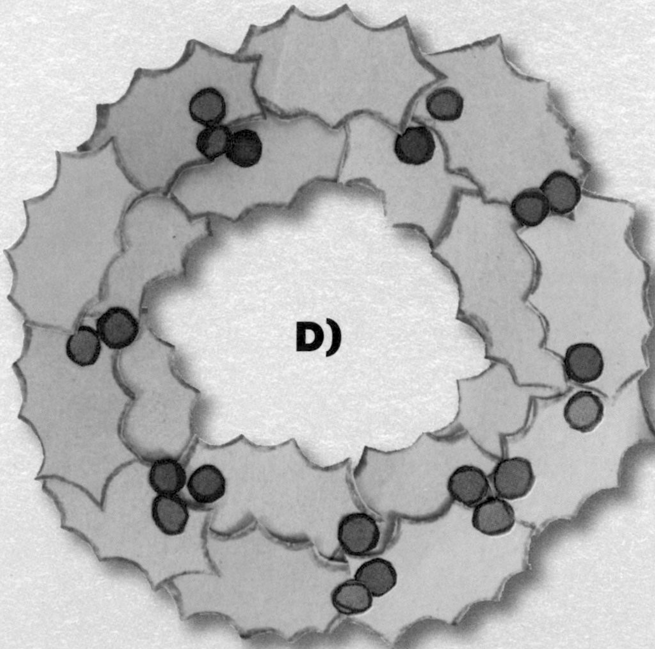

D)

5. Use about 6 inches of ribbon to a make a loop. Tape the loop of ribbon to the top and back of the wreath to hang it by (See E).

6. Use about 18 inches of ribbon to make a bow and glue it on the wreath as you wish (See F). Let dry.

E)

7. Ask an **adult** to help you hang the wreath.

F)

LITTLE SANTA

Almost every culture that celebrates Christmas has a special character that brings gifts to good children. In Italy a little old lady named La Befana brings the presents. In France a man named Père Noël brings the gifts. In England it is Father Christmas, in Holland it is Sint Niklaas, and in America it is Santa Claus. The American Santa Claus is usually dressed in a warm red snow suit and cap trimmed with white fur. He is rather plump and has a long white beard.

WHAT YOU WILL NEED

- tracing paper
- pencil
- white card stock
- scissors
- markers or crayons
- white glue
- clear tape

WHAT TO DO

1. Use tracing paper to transfer the pattern from page 38 to the white card stock. Cut out the pattern (See A).

A)

B)

2. Decorate both sides of the figure with markers or crayons as you wish (See B).

3. Pull the two flat sides of the body into the center and overlap them about a 1/4 inch. Glue or tape the overlap together (See C). Let dry.

4. Stand your Santa up and use him with other Christmas decorations.

c)

Pop-Up Chimney Card

A legend said that Saint Nicholas placed coins and other small presents in stockings that poor children had left by a fire to dry. Clement Clarke Moore's famous poem "A Visit From Saint Nicholas" described for the first time Santa Claus sliding down a chimney to leave presents in stockings that are hung by the fireplace. Here is a chimney with a Santa sliding down to make your Christmas merry.

What you will need

- white card stock
- tracing paper
- pencil
- scissors
- markers or crayons
- white glue
- construction paper

What to do

1. Fold a piece of white card stock in half width-wise, like a book. Use tracing paper to transfer the pattern from page 36 to the folded white card stock. Cut along the solid black lines of the pattern (See A).

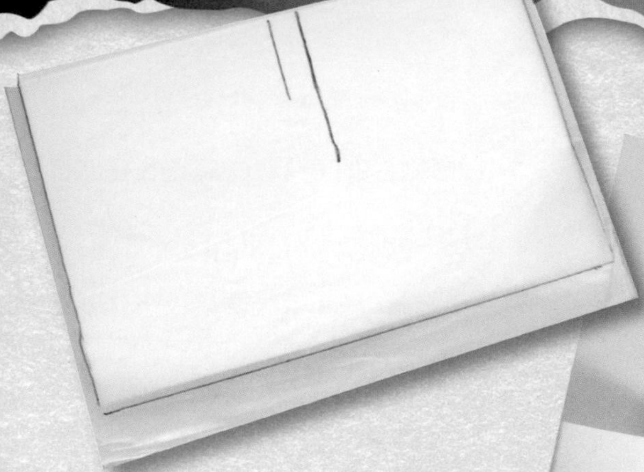

A)

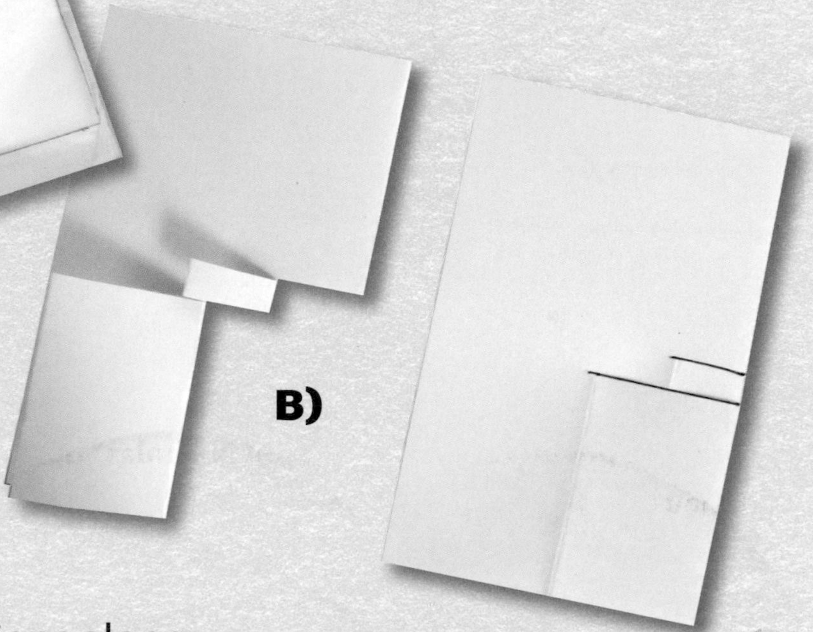

B)

2. Fold the cut sections along the fold lines and crease the fold with your finger. Put the cut sections back where they started (See B).

3. Open the folded card stock like a tent and push the cut sections down. Crease the paper on the folds again (See C).

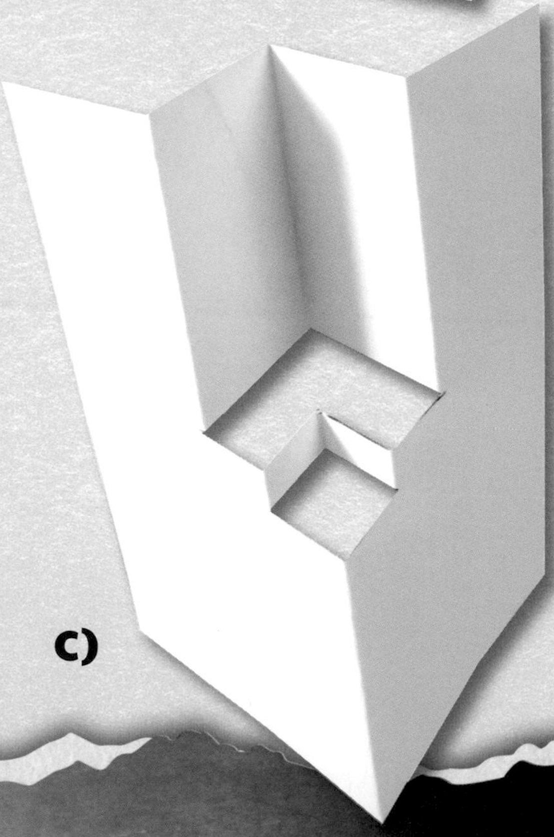

C)

4. Decorate the inside of the card with markers or crayons to look like a chimney and rooftop at night (See D).

D)

E)

5. Use tracing paper to transfer the Santa figure on page 35 to the card stock paper. Decorate the Santa figure with markers or crayons. Cut it out along the solid black lines (See E).

F)

I hope that you have been good, because...

6. Glue a sheet of construction paper to the outside edges of the back of the pop-up card. Let it dry. On the outside, write a Christmas message as you wish (See F).

7. Fold the Santa lengthwise and glue him onto the small pop-up section above the chimney. Let dry (See G).

Santa's coming! Merry Christmas!

G)

Santa's Reindeer

Reindeer are animals of the far north of Europe, Asia, and North America. They are especially good at running through the snow. They can be trained to pull sleighs over snowy roads and fields. No wonder they were chosen to be the animals to help Santa through the cold and snowy Christmas night.

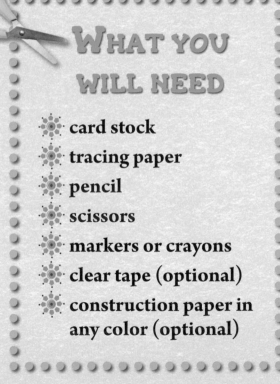

What You Will Need

- card stock
- tracing paper
- pencil
- scissors
- markers or crayons
- clear tape (optional)
- construction paper in any color (optional)

What To Do

1. Fold the card stock in half lengthwise.

2. Use tracing paper to transfer the pattern from page 40 to the folded card stock (See A). Cut out the pattern along the solid black lines.

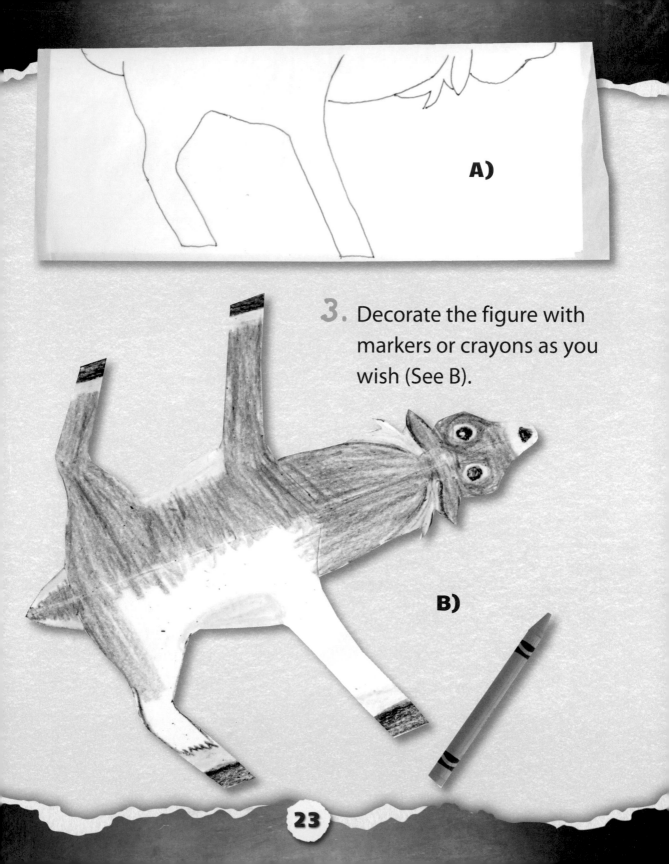

A)

3. Decorate the figure with markers or crayons as you wish (See B).

B)

4. Fold the figure along the fold lines as indicated.

5. Stand the finished reindeer up on its four legs. If you wish, use tape to fasten the reindeer to a piece of construction paper as a base.

"Look Who's Been Good!" Ornament

What you will need

- tracing paper
- pencil
- light cardboard
- scissors
- aluminum foil
- clear tape
- white glue
- photograph (Ask permission first!)
- glitter glue
- string

Ornaments are the decorations on a Christmas tree. Originally, Christmas trees were decorated with apples, nuts, and other goodies. Later, pretty glass balls and little toys and figures were added as decorations. Many families have favorite ornaments that they put on their Christmas tree year after year. The most special ornaments are those that remind us of past Christmases together. An ornament with your picture on it will be a special keepsake for years to come.

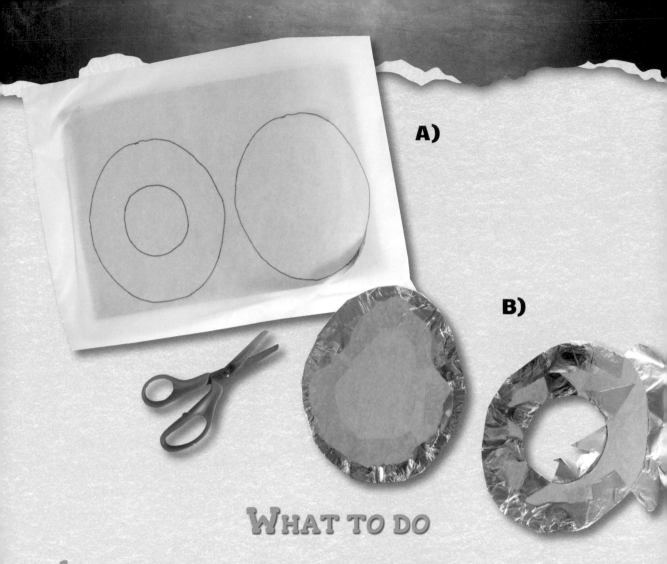

A)

B)

WHAT TO DO

1. Use tracing paper to transfer the ornament patterns from page 39 to a piece of light cardboard (See A).

2. Cut the patterns out of the cardboard. One piece will be solid and the other will have a hole in the center. Cover one side of each cardboard pattern piece with aluminum foil. Tape the loose edges of the foil in place (See B).

3. On the solid piece, glue a photograph of yourself in the center (See C). Let dry.

4. Place the other piece with the hole over the photograph to frame it. Glue it in place and let dry.

c)

5. Use glitter glue to decorate the ornament as you wish (See D). Let dry. Tie a 6-inch piece of string into a loop. Tape the string to the back of the ornament to hang it by (See E).

D)

E)

FALLING SNOWFLAKES

Snow covers much of the northern United States and Canada in December. Many people like a snowy, white Christmas. Snow is formed high in the clouds when moisture in the air starts to freeze into a frost. A snowflake always has six sides. Each snowflake is different from any other snowflake.

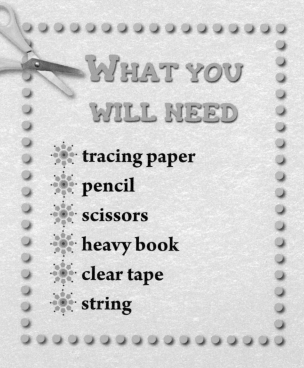

WHAT YOU WILL NEED

- tracing paper
- pencil
- scissors
- heavy book
- clear tape
- string

WHAT TO DO

1. Use tracing paper to copy the pattern on page 42. Copy the letters and numbers on the pattern as shown. Cut out the pattern from the tracing paper (See A).

A)

2. Fold the pattern in half so that corner A1 meets A2 and corner B1 meets B2.

3. Fold corner C2 up to the A corner. Fold corner C1 up to the B corner (See B).

4. Fold the B corner over to meet the A corner. This makes a right triangle (See C).

B)

C)

D)

5. Cut little shapes out of each side of the triangle. Be careful not to cut all the way across the triangle (See D). There are patterns suggested on page 43.

6. Gently unfold the paper to find the six-sided snowflake design. Set it under a heavy book or weight for a few hours to press it flat.

7. Use clear tape and string to hang your snowflake **with an adult's help** (See E).

E)

PAPER PLATE ANGEL

Angels are heavenly messengers. They are often shown with wings to show that they can fly. The night that Jesus was born, angels filled the skies above the fields of Palestine, the land that is now called Israel, to tell the shepherds the happy news. Angel figures are popular decorations at Christmas time.

WHAT YOU WILL NEED

- thin 9-inch paper plate
- tracing paper
- pencil
- scissors
- markers or crayons
- clear tape

WHAT TO DO

1. Fold the paper plate in half.

2. Use tracing paper to transfer the pattern on page 41 to the folded paper plate (See A). Cut out the pattern.

A)

3. Lay the angel figure out flat and decorate it with markers or crayons as you wish (See B).

B)

C)

4. Fold the angel figure along the fold lines as shown (See C).

D)

5. Overlap the ends of the angel's gown together behind the angel about 3/4 of an inch and tape them together (See D).

6. Set the angel on a table or counter for a decoration, or **ask an adult** to put it on a Christmas tree.

PATTERNS

Use tracing paper to copy the patterns on these pages.
Ask an adult to help you cut and trace the shapes.

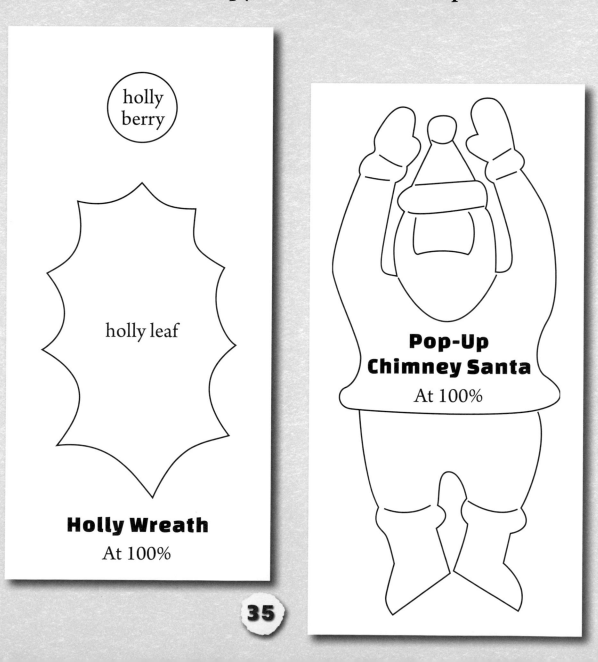

holly
berry

holly leaf

Holly Wreath
At 100%

**Pop-Up
Chimney Santa**
At 100%

Pop-Up Chimney Card

Enlarge to 115%

O Christmas Tree

Enlarge to 115%

X

X

X

Staple along the X's

X

X

X

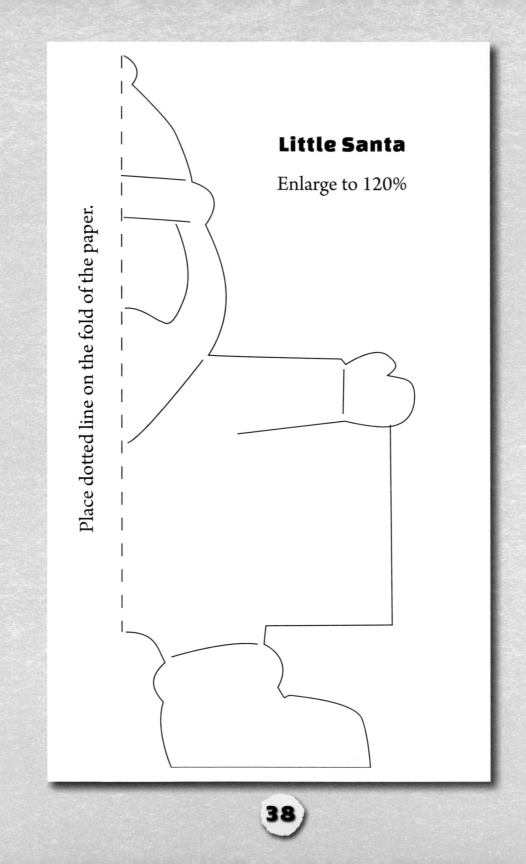

Little Santa

Enlarge to 120%

Place dotted line on the fold of the paper.

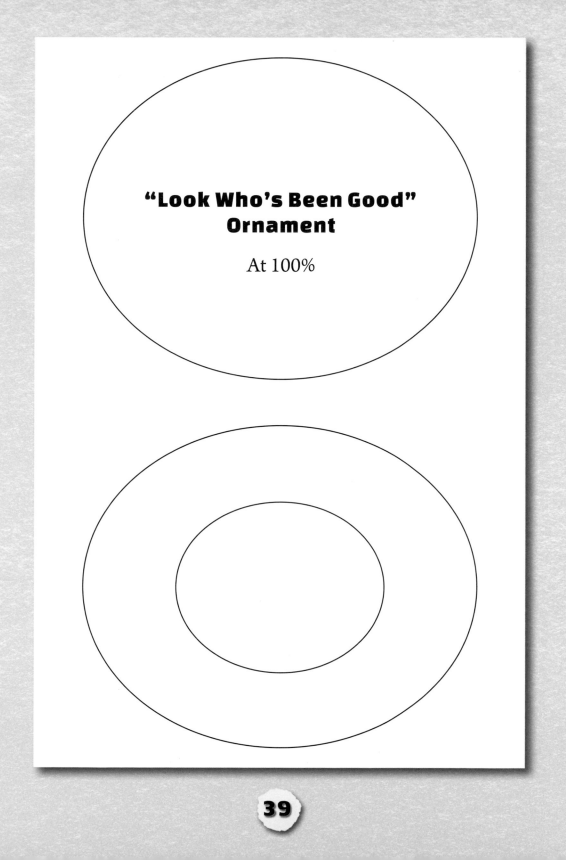

"Look Who's Been Good"
Ornament

At 100%

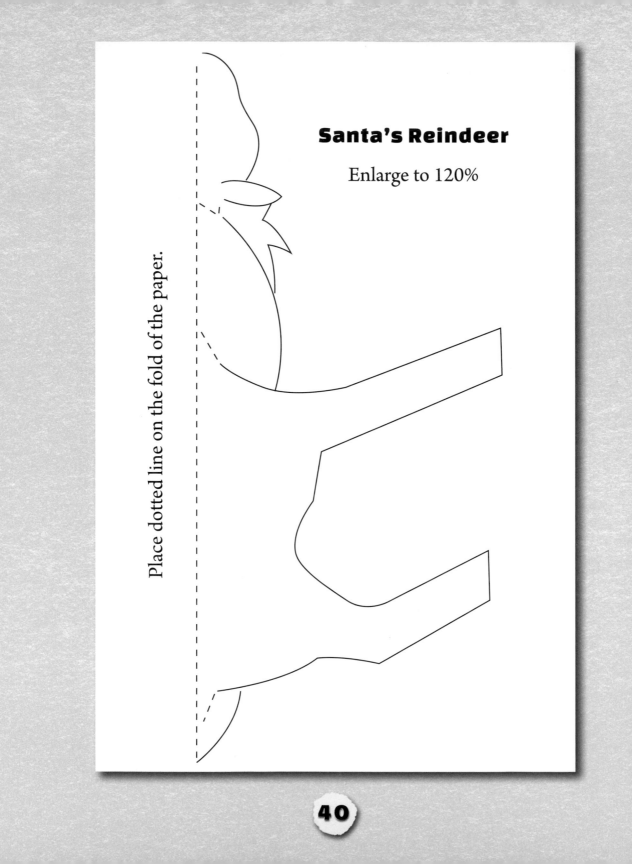

Santa's Reindeer

Enlarge to 120%

Place dotted line on the fold of the paper.

Paper Plate Angel

Enlarge to 115%

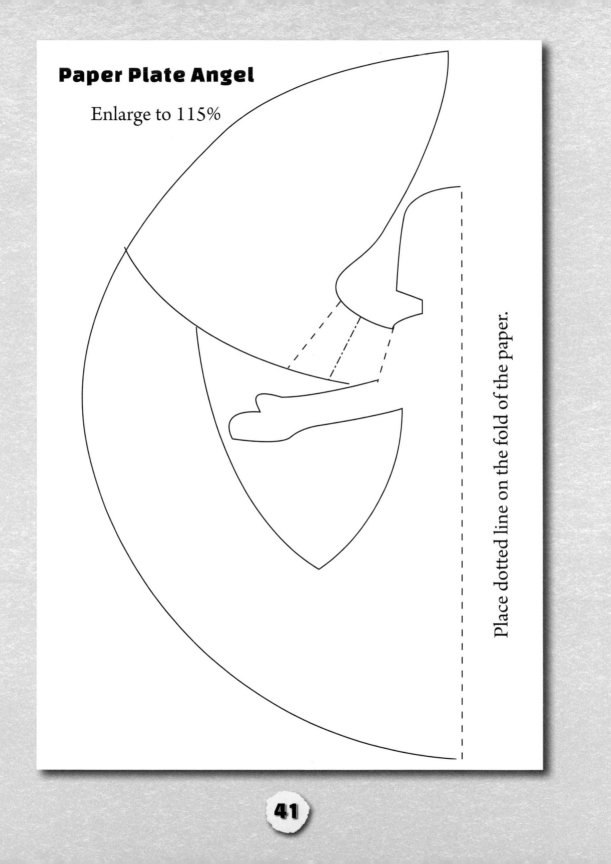

Place dotted line on the fold of the paper.

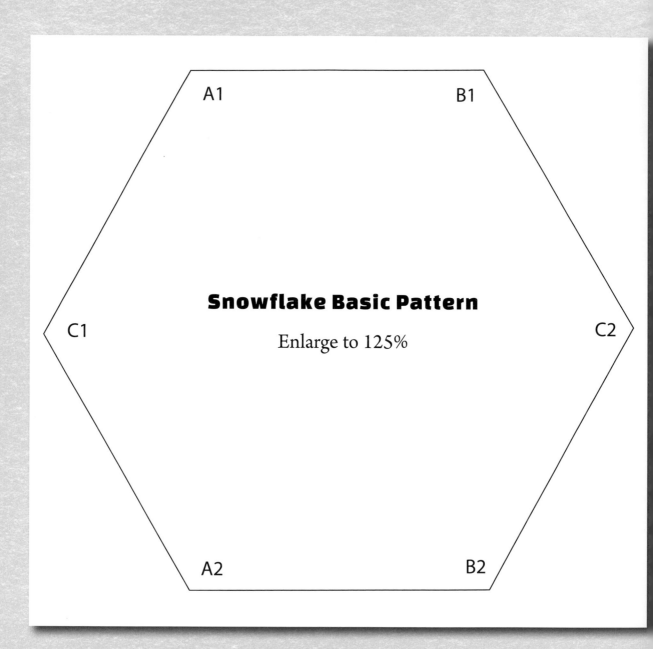

Snowflake Basic Pattern

Enlarge to 125%

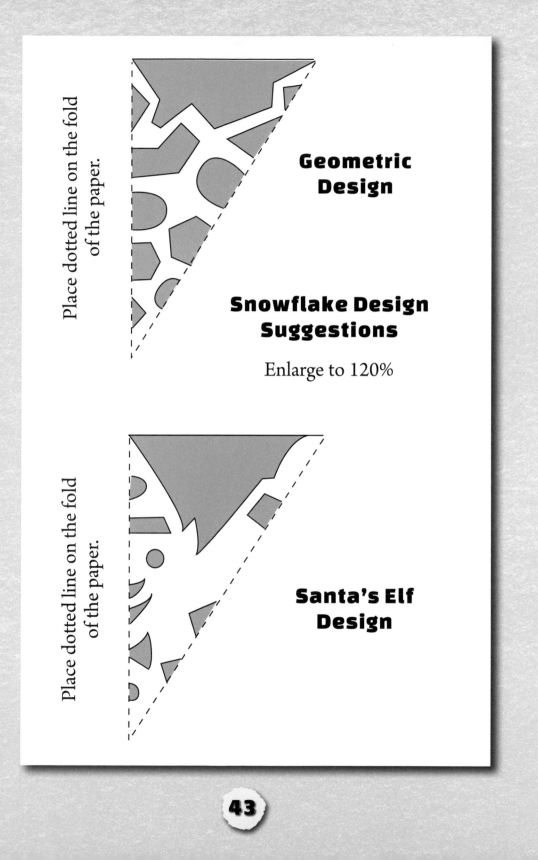

Place dotted line on the fold of the paper.

Geometric Design

Snowflake Design Suggestions

Enlarge to 120%

Place dotted line on the fold of the paper.

Santa's Elf Design

READ ABOUT

Bronson, Linda. *Sleigh Bells and Snowflakes: A Celebration of Christmas.* New York: Henry Holt and Company, 2002.

Kaner, Etta. *Who Likes the Snow?* Toronto, Canada: Kids Can Press, 2006.

Lankford, Mary. D. *Christmas USA.* New York: Collins, 2006.

Moore, Clement Clarke. *The Night Before Christmas.* New York: Marshall Cavendish, 2006.

Rosinsky, Natalie M. *Christmas.* Minneapolis, Minn.: Compass Point Books, 2003.

Visit Randel McGee's Web site at

http://www.mcgeeproductions.com

INDEX

About the Author

Randel McGee has been playing with paper and scissors for as long as he can remember. As soon as he was able to get a library card, he would go to the library and find the books that showed paper crafts, check them out, take them home, and try almost every craft in the book. He still checks out books on paper crafts at the library, but he also buys books to add to his own library and researches paper-craft sites on the Internet.

McGee says, "I begin by making copies of simple crafts or designs I see in books. Once I get the idea of how something is made, I begin to make changes to make the designs more personal. After a lot of trial and error, I find ways to do something new and different that is all my own. That's when the fun begins!"

McGee also liked singing and acting from a young age. He graduated college with a degree in children's theater and specialized in puppetry. After college, he taught himself ventriloquism and started performing at libraries and schools with a friendly dragon puppet named Groark.

"Randel McGee and Groark" have toured throughout the United States and Asia, sharing their fun shows with young and old alike. Groark is the star of two award-winning video series for elementary school students on character education: *Getting Along with Groark* and *The Six Pillars of Character.*

In the 1990s, McGee combined his love of making things with paper with his love of telling stories. He tells stories while making pictures cut from paper to illustrate the tales he tells. The famous author Hans Christian Andersen also made cut-paper pictures when he told stories. McGee portrays Andersen in storytelling performances around the world.

Besides performing and making things, McGee, with the help of his wife, Marsha, likes showing librarians, teachers, fellow artists, and children the fun and educational experiences they can have with paper crafts, storytelling, drama, and puppetry. Randel McGee has belonged to the Guild of American Papercutters, the National Storytelling Network, and the International Ventriloquists' Association. He has been a regional director for the Puppeteers of America, Inc., and past president of UNIMA-USA, an international puppetry organization. He has been active in working with children and scouts in his community and church for many years. He and his wife live in California. They are the parents of five grown children who are all talented artists and performers.